THE ART AND CRAFT OF
Goldwork

ANTONIA LOMNY

The Art and Craft of Goldwork
First published in Australia in 2004 by
Simon & Schuster (Australia) Pty Limited
14-16 Suakin Street
Suite 2, Lower Ground Floor
Pymble, NSW 2073

A Viacom Company
Sydney New York London Toronto

Visit our website at www.simonsaysaustralia.com

© Antonia Lomny, 2004

All rights reserved. No part of this publication may be reproduced, sorted in a retrieval
system, or transmitted, in any form or by any means, electronic, mechanical, photocopying,
recording or otherwise, without the prior permission of the publisher in writing.

Lomny, Antonia.
     The art and craft of goldwork.

     ISBN 0 7318 1217 4.

     1. Gold embroidery. 2. Gold thread. 3. Goldwork -
Handbooks, manuals, etc. I. Title.

     746.44028

Cover and internal design by Warren Ventures
Typeset in 10.5/15pt Galliard
Printed in China through Colorcraft Ltd, Hong Kong

10 9 8 7 6 5 4 3 2 1

Contents

Acknowledgments

This book would not exist without the help of a large number of people. First and foremost, thanks must go to two friends, Clare Wallis and Susan Gower. Clare encouraged me to submit a proposal, and Susan, an avid goldworker herself, supported me when the proposal was actually accepted. Susan's work can be seen in Project 4. My thanks also go to Nick Gower, who worked tirelessly on my hand drawings to provide an excellent set of templates.

Alison Snepp, of Mosman Needlecraft, was another great supporter whose wise counsel saved me from many missteps. Her guidance was invaluable. I would like to also thank my two excellent goldwork teachers, Avril Ambrose De Haviland and June Fiford, whose enthusiasm, skill and encouragement helped fire my imagination. Thanks must also go to my stylist, Louise Owens, and photographer, Andre Martin. Their eye for colour and detail enhanced the work immeasurably.

I would also like to warmly acknowledge the support that only friends and family can give. My profound thanks must go to my husband, Bill (who said all along that this is what I really should be doing!), and our dear friends Anna and Lloyd, Lis and Ian, and Karen and Vic. Professional support came unstintingly from within the Blue Mountains arts community in Blackheath, especially the Stop Laughing This is Serious Gallery, John Martin from Jed's Place, and Dennis Andrews from Cambria Books.

Preface

The beauty of goldwork has long fascinated me. The lustre of the gold threads, when combined with richly hued silks, lush velvets and gold, pearl and glass beads, is breathtaking. Goldwork, with its roots in ecclesiastical needlework, evokes not only the richness of old churches but an air of quiet meditation. I prefer setting aside a full morning or afternoon for goldwork, as this gives me time to settle into a rhythm.

The creation of a piece of goldwork is not difficult. The main technique for laying gold threads against a piece of cloth is using a couching (or anchoring) stitch, which secures the threads at small regular intervals. Once the couching technique is mastered, there is no end to what you can do with the many gold threads available.

The flexibility of the gold thread makes it ideal for defining or highlighting any line design you wish to use, while massed gold thread can create shimmering areas of gold that catch the light in a variety of patterns.

The couching thread itself can help to create further patterns in your design. Usually a thin gold-coloured thread is used to couch the gold threads down. By varying the spacing of the couching stitch you are able to create subtle patterns, such as brickwork in massed square shapes or wheel spokes in a circle of laid gold threads. By introducing coloured silks, you can add subtle shading and even delineate pictures in a massed block of gold thread.

While most of the gold (metal) threads are laid on the fabric, there are also gold threads that can pass through cloth repeatedly. Gold embroidery can be used in conjunction with laid gold thread to achieve designs of great subtlety, capturing light and shadow.

The designs in this book are inspired by some of my most favourite periods of the fine and decorative arts. I have lectured on eighteenth and nineteenth-century decorative arts for more than ten years after studying with Christie's auction house in London in the late 1980s. The decoration of furniture, silver, glass, ceramics and needlecrafts of the ages is a great source of inspiration to me.

By choosing the right thread for the right type of work — for instance, using smooth purl and couched threads for work that will be handled often — goldwork can feature as giftware, such as the Monsoon Wedding gift bag (Project 13), Japanese-style damascened needle case (Project 3), the Belle Epoch notebook cover (Project 6) and some fun Christmas decorations (Project 15).

Various fashion accessories, such as earrings (Project 11), dramatic bracelets (Project 10), elegant hair clips (Project 4), velvet wrap trims (Project 5) and funky handbags (Project 14), can also be enhanced with goldwork designs.

Goldwork can further beautify your home. William Morris (1834–1896) advocated 'Have nothing in your houses which you do not know to be useful or believe to be beautiful.' Goldwork pictures of eighteenth-century style flowers (Project 12), ancient Egyptian swirls (Project 7) and the Medieval Goldwork Sampler (Project 1) can enliven the darkest corner. Three-dimensional homewares can also benefit from decorative goldwork designs, such as a goldwork frame (Project 9), a lampshade (Project 8) and a delightful miniature heart to hang over your bed (Project 2).

May goldwork become a way of life for you, giving you inspiration to devote time to the creation of beauty.

ANTONIA LOMNY

The different types of gold thread

There are a variety of threads that can be used in goldwork. These include the following (which will be the mainstays of the designs within this book):

JAPANESE GOLD

This thread, also known as 'Jap gold' or 'Jap thread', is made from thin strips of gold coloured paper, about 1 mm (1/24 inch) wide, which are wrapped around a continuous strand of fibre. It is mainly available either as Substitute Jap or Imitation Jap. Substitute Jap has a glittery gold colour and is available in sizes preceded by the letter 'K' and a number. The smaller the number, the thicker the thread; for example, 'K4' is a medium-sized thread that is used for a variety of designs, while K2 is a thicker thread that can be used in heavier designs. Imitation Jap is softer in colour and easier to manipulate. It is also available in a variety of thicknesses — in particular for the designs in this book, T70 and T71. I love the massed effect of T71 (see Project 3), which I find easy to twist and turn in tight corners, making beautiful massed shapes.

TWIST

This thread is made from twisted strands of Jap thread and is delightfully easy to manipulate around curves. It is available in a number of thicknesses. A 3-ply twist is a medium-sized twist suitable for goldwork, which passes through fabric quite easily. Some thicker twists are harder to pass through fabric and may need to be finished by sewing couching thread a number of times around the ends so that they will not fray. Twist threads are available in gold, white gold, silver and a limited range of colours, such as burgundy, green, purple and blue.

PURLS

Smooth purl

Smooth purl is a hollow, tightly coiled wire thread, of which small segments are stitched to fabric to form a filling that looks like shiny raised satin stitch. Smooth purl commonly comes in sizes such as #5 or #6. Less commonly available, but still possible to order, are size #8, which is usually much thinner, and #2, which is much thicker.

Rough purl

This is a hollow thread with a matt sheen, which is used in the same way as smooth purl. It comes in the same sizes and is available in a limited range of colours.

Bright check purl

This is also a hollow tubular metal thread that is like a twist of very thin square coils of wire. This is an excellent, highly textured thread that can be couched in rows or in a random scatterings of small segments that make up a shimmering infill of gold (see Project 1).

Pearl purl

This is gold-plated wire that is tightly coiled with a hollow centre. It is usually stretched to 1½ times its length and couched invisibly onto the fabric in between its coils, which look like a string of small gold beads. Pearl purl comes in a variety of thicknesses, such as very fine, #1 (fine), #2 (medium, and the most commonly used type), and #3 (thick). It is also available in gold, silver and copper. It is an excellent thread for outlining shapes in a goldwork design.

JACOBEAN THREAD AND PASSING THREADS

These fine gold threads are the only ones that can pass continuously through fabric without fraying, and can be used to work a variety of embroidery stitches, such as chain stitch, French knot and a number of interesting woven stitches, including the raised stem band (see below; Medieval Palace Sampler (Project 1) and the Ethnic Goldwork Bracelet (Project 10)). Jacobean Thread is also referred to as No 30 thread. Passing threads come in a variety of thicknesses (No 4 is a thin thread, while No 13 is fairly thick) and qualities, such as smooth or wavy. Some experienced goldwork embroiderers even use thin passing threads as couching thread. I like to use them as a delicate repeated pattern couched down with gold coloured silk couching thread (see the Dream of Summer Butterflies Lampshade (Project 8)).

How to sew a raised stem band

You will require Jacobean thread, about 46 cm (18 inches) long, threaded onto a chenille needle (No 18). In the area that is to be filled, such as the diamonds and triangles in the Ethnic Goldwork Bracelet (Project 10), sew a series of stitches, 3 mm (1/8 inches) apart, covering the shape, like bars on a prison window or rungs on a ladder. These stitches will be the base for the woven stitch. Bring your needle up into one corner of the diamond, preferably on the bottom left-hand side (if you are right-handed).

Then move your needle over and under the first bar, making a loop with the Jacobean thread. Do this again over the second bar and continue until the end of the row. Sink your needle in the bottom right-hand corner and bring the needle up again just above your first row on the left-hand side. Continue weaving your Jacobean thread over the 'bars' or 'rungs' until you completely fill the area. As some of your shapes are irregular, your rungs will diminish as you progress with the filling. Simply continue until you have no rungs left, ensuring that each row appears to begin and end flush with the edge of the shape. After each row, use the blunt end of your needle or a mellor (see standard goldwork kit) to make sure that each woven line sits snugly against the previous one.

Framing up at the start

Once you have decided which design you would like to try, and have enlarged, traced or otherwise prepared your template, choose the background fabric or fabrics for your work. Rich, strongly coloured cloth or fabrics that give the appearance of being shot with gold or silver can work very effectively against gold threads. Silks and velvets are the usual choice.

If using a thin fabric, such as silk, it is important to stabilise the fabric by stitching it onto calico, which has already been stretched onto a frame. Heavy velvets can be stretched directly onto the frame.

Use a light-weight tapestry frame (see Suppliers on page 63) and measure up your calico so that the fabric is slightly larger than the frame. Fold and stitch down the edges of the calico so that it fits within the frame, leaving approximately 2.5 cm (1 inch) of space along the width and 2.5 cm (1 inch) of extra calico along the length.

Your frame will have a piece of cloth taped along the top and bottom arm of the frame. Mark the centre of the tape with a sharp pencil. Fold the width of your calico in half and mark the middle of the top and bottom edges. Match the marks and sew the calico using an overstitch, spaced about 3 mm (⅛ inch) apart or less.

Once you have stitched the calico onto the tape, roll the top and bottom arms of the frame so that the calico is slightly stretched. Tighten the butterfly wings to hold the stretch. You may wish to purchase a frame 'tightener', which is a small oblong piece of wood that has a slit in the middle of one side. This side fits neatly over the butterfly wings of most frames and helps you tighten the work during its progress.

Using natural string, such as kitchen twine, threaded onto a long, sturdy needle with a generous-sized eye, sew the twine into the side of the calico and then loop it over the side arm of the frame. Do this all the way down the side of the calico and the frame, spacing the stitches about 3.5 cm (1½ inches) apart. You may need to use pliers to get the thick twine through the double fold of calico along the sides.

One end of the twine can be stitched several times at different angles into the calico. Slightly tighten the tension of the threads along the edge, looping the other end of the thread around either the butterfly nut or in a figure eight pattern on a long pin positioned at an angle in the corner of the fabric.

At this stage, the calico should only be slightly stretched. Position your background fabric onto the calico and stitch it down using either a herringbone stitch or a series of short and long stitches perpendicular to the edge of the fabric. Always start at the middle of each edge, working towards the outer corner and smoothing the fabric down so that it is lying flat on the calico.

When you are ready, tighten the arms of the frame and the threads along the side. The fabric should now be stretched drum tight. Check that there are no ripples in your fabric. If there are, lighten the tension of the fabric, and re-sew the background fabric onto the calico. Retighten the fabric. If you are making a goldwork handbag, velvet wrap, cushion or other unframed work, you may wish to tack a piece of fabric stiffener to the back of the fabric. When satisfied, you are ready to transfer your design onto the fabric (see page 12).

Transferring a design

One of my favourite ways of transferring a design is by stitching a rough outline of the pattern onto the fabric. I have used this technique for all the designs in this book, particularly as some of the design lines are quite intricate. Templates are included for each design. In most cases you will need to resize the design to your requirements. Once you are happy with the size of your design, you will need to transfer it to your fabric.

To use this technique, trace the design onto soft tissue paper and then stitch the tissue paper where you wish the pattern to appear on your fabric. First, stitch down the tissue paper so that it is lying flat on the fabric. To do this, use large tacking stitches to sew down the centre of the design and then across the centre so that you have a large cross shape. If you are tacking down a medium to large design, you may also wish to stitch along the diagonals, so that a star pattern is tacked across the design.

Now you are ready to stitch the outline of the design. Use a thread that stands out against the colour of your fabric. I like using yellow-coloured cotton thread that will not show up as prominently beneath the gold thread.

Do not make the tacking stitches outlining the design too wide, as when you tear the paper the stitches will be pulled up, creating a bit of a loop. If this occasionally happens, all you need to do is pull the thread back onto the fabric from the back of the work.

You do not need to follow slavishly each line of the work, particularly in this book. Sometimes it will be enough simply to indicate on your work where a circle or a central motif should be positioned, such as in the Elizabethan Heart-shaped Miniature Cushion (Project 2) and the Japanese-style Damascened Needle Case (Project 3). This is also the case with regard to scrolls or looping of gold thread, such as those in the Medieval Palace Goldwork Sampler (Project 1) or the Folk Art Goldwork Frame (Project 9).

I find the paper of dressmaking patterns particularly useful for transferring a goldwork design. It is soft enough to tear and transparent enough for you to see the design under the paper very easily. If you are a dressmaker, you may find that you have a number of patterns that are out of date or were a mistake in the first place. Cull your collection of patterns and consider recycling the tissue paper for your goldwork. I find patterns for larger items, such as dresses, dressing gowns and capes, particularly useful.

TIP

When the pattern is stitched, run the point of your needle along the stitching line.
This will make it easier to remove the paper.

Goldwork techniques

WORKING WITH GOLD THREADS

As soon as you get your Jap gold and twist threads home, it is a good idea to store them on a soft roll of felt. Make up one roll for each type of gold thread you have. As you will regularly couch your Jap gold and thin twists in pairs, you may wind these threads in two coils on the one felt roll.

Making felt rolls is very simple. All you need is a couple of sheets of felt which you can purchase ready-cut in craft shops. Cut one sheet in half (or to whatever size you want) and roll the felt tightly. Sew the end of the roll down with tiny stitches, securing the ends.

Gold thread is often sold on a reel, in acid-free tissue paper or in acid-free plastic bags. Using ordinary plastic bags for your gilt goldwork threads must be avoided at all costs. If improperly handled or stored, the gold threads — particularly the hollow varieties, such as pearl purl, bright check and the smooth or rough purl — may tarnish. When you unwind the gold thread from its packaging, make sure you do not crimp the thread and be very careful to get any potential kink out of the thread.

Jap gold and twist threads must be unwound from their packaging onto the felt roll. Purchase a number of sheets of acid-free tissue paper. These are not very expensive and are available from most art supplies stores. Wrap each felt roll of gold threads with the tissue paper. Store your rolls in cardboard boxes. If you are fond of stationery, this is a great excuse to get a box for each type of goldwork thread — Jap gold and twist could fit in one box, all your pearl purl can reside in another box, while your smooth, rough and bright check purls can be stored in another.

You will also need to take extra care of your hands when dealing with goldwork. Goldwork is best done with extremely clean and dry hands. If you tend towards oiliness in your fingers, handle your threads only when necessary, using tweezers whenever possible.

My hands tend towards dryness so my main problem is having the metal in the threads slightly tear at my fingers. This can be most annoying, as the tiny tears catch the silk couching thread, weakening it. After my goldworking session, I use heavy-duty hand cream (a British cream called E 45 is superb for very dry hands) before I go to bed, allowing the cream to soak into my skin, replenishing the moisture and healing the tears. Do not use hand cream immediately before working on your goldwork and keep your hands clean while working with your gold threads and wires.

COUCHING TECHNIQUES

Lines of goldwork threads, such as gold Jap, twist and pearl purl, are couched onto the background fabric to create design lines or areas of massed, textured gold. Couching is a very easy technique to master. It is simply a small stitch sewn through the background fabric to capture the goldwork thread in the required position. The stitch should be at right angles to and the same width as the thread. Extremely fine, hollow goldwork threads or wires, such as smooth and rough purl and bright check, are usually cut to length and the silk is threaded through the wire. Sometimes a couching stitch is used to secure the top end of a loop of smooth or rough purl (such as petals of the gold flower in Project 12).

Different types of couching thread

There are various types of thread that can be used for couching and they are available in a variety of colours. The easiest to use is a fine 100% silk thread (for example, all the work done for this book was couched using silk thread #50 distributed by the YLI Corporation). Usually, silk of the same colour as the gold is used (the couching thread used in this book is #50 – 078 from YLI).

Metallic threads can also be used for couching. YLI distributes a metallic yarn. No 601 is an almost white gold colour, which has a pleasant effect against twist threads that are also white gold. A German thread called Metallic Madeira can be used, in particular No 40, gold-7. DMC distributes a metallic thread made in France, called Fil métallisé, that can be used for couching. A single thread of Fil métallisé is made up of three much thinner threads. These are very delicate and can be used to couch thin strands of gold twist.

Use short lengths of these couching threads, as they do tend to fray or split, particularly when you are working with the gold wires. I like to use lengths between 20 cm (8 inches) and 30 cm (12 inches). One way of keeping the thread relatively undamaged during the couching process is to lightly slide a small amount of beeswax along the thread. Needlework suppliers usually carry beeswax that is specially packaged in a circular plastic container with convenient slits on the edge so that it is quick and easy to run a thread along the edge of the beeswax inside the container. Waxing strengthens the thread and should be

done especially when couching pearl purl and basketwork stitches.

Strands of coloured silk, and other thin embroidery threads, can also be used to couch down gold thread. A goldwork technique called Or Nue calls for using coloured thread to couch tightly packed rows of gold thread. Beautifully shaded patterns can emerge from this technique. We have introduced a simplified version (using only one colour of thread but picking the pattern out by varying the spacing of the couching thread) in the Medieval Palace Goldwork Sampler (Project 1).

> Instructions for other useful goldwork techniques, such as padding, embroidery and the incorporation of beads, palettes and chains into your work, will be explained on an individual project basis.

Basic couching

Cut your couching thread into a 20 cm (8 inch) length and thread it through a needle with a narrow eye. I like to use No 11 Sharps (John James, Article No L4310). Run the thread along your piece of beeswax. Make sure that no blobs of wax are left on the thread. Tie a knot at the end of your thread.

With a fabric marker, draw a line on your calico, which has been framed up according to the instructions on page 11. Sew up through the background fabric at the point where your line starts and sew a couching stitch onto the calico. Position your gold thread on the line, leaving about 2.5 cm (1 inch) tail.

Sew up through the fabric so that the needle comes up above the gold thread close to the beginning of the line. Now sew your couching thread down close below the gold thread, making sure that the couching stitch is exactly perpendicular to the gold thread. Repeat the same stitch about 3 mm (⅛ inch) further along the line. Continue until you finish your line.

It is important not to nick the gold thread with your needle and to sew the couching thread lightly so that the gold thread stays on your drawn line. With just a little bit of practice you will be able to couch very straight lines and to progress to the most intricate of lines. Projects that allow you to practise couching straight lines include the Medieval Palace Goldwork Sampler (Project 1) and the Belle Epoch Notebook Cover (Project 6).

One of the best ways to couch a straight line of gold thread is to secure the thread with one or two couching stitches at the beginning of the line and then stretch out the gold thread or threads with your fingers of your left hand (if you are right-handed) or your right hand (if you are left-handed). This will help you position your couching stitches. In the beginning, you may want to use a flexible ruler that measures out millimetres, so that you can make sure that your stitches are exactly 3 mm (⅛ inch) apart. Soon you will be able to see that your couching thread is correctly spaced.

When couching a second line of gold thread or threads above the first line, butt the gold threads close to the first thread and couch stitches along the second line so that they fall between the couching stitches along the first line. As you add more and more lines, your couching stitches will form a 'brickwork' pattern. For practice in making a block of gold threads, see the Japanese-style Damascened Needle Case (Project 3).

Often two strands of gold Jap or twist are stitched so that they lay side to side against the background fabric. One couching thread secures two threads in position. For a more delicate look, I like using just a single strand of

gold thread, usually twist, as I find a single Jap gold thread looks slightly insubstantial for larger designs.

You may wish to start your couching from the left (if you are right-handed) or from the right (if you are left-handed). Try to make sure that your couching thread sits perpendicular to the thread you are couching and that it does not slant.

TIP

If you are not happy with your couching, check the tension of your fabric. The fabric needs to be drum tight. Loose fabric is the major cause of poor couching.

Cutting gold thread and sinking the ends

When you have finished your line, cut the gold thread so that a tail of 2.5 cm (1 inch) is left. With your couching thread, sew a tiny stitch into the calico near the end of the drawn line and leave your couching thread hanging from the needle on the underside of your work. Keep the needle and thread away from the end. Sink a chenille needle through the point where you want your gold thread to end, leaving the eye and part of the needle shank showing above the fabric. Carefully thread the gold thread tail through the eye and with a quick tug pull the thread through to the underside of the fabric.

It is always an idea to hold down the gold thread gently with one hand as you tug the thread through the fabric with the other. The shorter the line of gold thread, the more likely it is to disappear entirely along with the needle to the underside of the fabric, leaving you with a row of loops of beautifully spaced couching and no gold thread!

Use your couching thread to sew down the tail of the gold thread along the underside of the line you have couched. So that it is not too bulky, you can thin down the gold thread by gently untwirling and cutting away the gold from the silk core thread.

The ends of a thread or threads can be staggered, especially around the outer rim of a circle, so that the ending of the threads is not too obvious.

Couching circles

When starting to couch a circle, sew two couching stitches over your gold thread or threads to secure the threads at the centre of the circle. Twirl the gold thread or threads around this central point, leaving the tail end of the thread to flop over the emerging circle. Start couching stitches to secure the circle of thread. The spacing of your couching thread will vary. Couching stitches for circles can be positioned in a pattern around the circle so that the stitches seem to form spokes of a wheel. For larger circles, this can leave stretches of gold thread wider than 3 mm (1/8 inch). I tend to keep the width of couching stitches from 1 mm (1/24 inch) (near the centre of the circle) to 3 mm (1/8 inch) for circles — see the Medieval Palace Goldwork Sampler (Project 1) and the Japanese-style Damascened Needle Case (Project 3).

Turning a corner: couching a square and filling spaces

To couch a square, you will need to turn corners with your gold thread. With some practice, you will find that turning a corner is not too arduous. Some threads turn corners better than others — heavier-gauge Jap gold is trickier to manipulate than thinner ones, such as T71 and T70. Twists can be bulky but turn corners beautifully.

To practise, try couching another line of gold thread (use two threads this time). At the end, rather than cutting the thread and sinking the ends, sew your couching thread through the fabric where you would like your gold thread or threads to turn. Using the taut couching thread as a guide, press your gold thread or threads against it, creating a bend in the gold thread. Lay the threads flat against the first line, going in the opposite direction, and sink the couching thread at the end of the turned corner, securing the turn. As mentioned earlier, position your couching stitches for the second line in between the stitches of the first line. An excellent project to help you practise turning your threads is the Merry Yule Christmas Ornaments (Project 15).

To form a square or rectangle, stitch along the outside of one side of the shape. At the

---

Making your own velvet-covered cardboard

Cut out a heavy piece of cardboard measuring 8 cm (3 inches) by 13 cm (5 inches). Cut out a piece of velvet (blue, black or red) so that it measures 13 cm (5 inches) by 18 cm (7 inches). Spray the underside of the velvet with an ozone-friendly spray adhesive that is suitable for fabrics (try a test piece of velvet first). Carefully position the cardboard in the middle of the fabric and turn the ends over the edge. Allow the velvet-covered cardboard to dry.

corner, turn the gold thread as described above and couch it down along the next side of the shape. Continue until you have outlined the shape entirely. At this point, you will start filling the shape with couched line within the outline. There are two types of filling you can use within a shape — solid filling and contour filling.

Unsurprisingly, a solid, massed filling of gold thread is characteristic of solid filling. Every line of couched gold thread is laid against another line of gold. At the corners, particularly as you get closer to the middle of the shape, you may find that the thread is too bulky to fit perfectly into the corner and that a space starts to occur. If you are couching two lines of gold thread, you can alleviate the spacing left in the corner by couching not two lines but one line at a time at the corner, pushing each single thread closer into the corner.

This is a useful technique when trying to fill in an irregular shape with couched line (see Dream of Summer Butterflies Tea Light Lampshade, Project 8). For some irregular shapes, a space will inevitably occur but you will notice that a rather attractive, almost filigree pattern can emerge as space is left in the corners.

Contour filling is a type of design with couched gold thread or threads that follow the outline of the shape in a diminishing pattern, leaving space in between the lines (see Folk Art Goldwork Frame, Project 9).

Couching pearl purl

Pearl purl is an excellent wire for lining shapes (see Medieval Palace Goldwork Sampler, Project 1). Pearl purl comes as a tightly wound wire with no room for couching thread to pass. You will need to pull the wire slightly apart so that couching thread can easily pass through the wire and secure the line of pearl purl to the background fabric. Usually pearl purl is stretched 1½ times its length. Pearl purl can be couched in lines (see the Belle Epoch Notebook Cover, Project 6) to create a striped effect. To couch a line of pearl purl, you will simply couch a stitch between every second or third loop.

I prefer not to precut the pearl purl but to leave it as a longer piece, as it makes it easier to handle. When you have reached the end, stop couching within four or six loops of the end, slide your scissors (a pair specially kept for cutting gold thread and wire) over the last loop and cut it so that the end of the wire is pointing into the background fabric.

To form a square, the wire can be bent as you get closer to corner. Sew two couching stitches in the same place at the corner.

Pearl purl can also be stretched out a bit further and twirled around tightly to create an interesting, evenly textured circle (see the Byzantine Empress Earrings, Project 11), and the Eclectic Goldwork Handbag, Project 14). You will need to couch down between every loop in the centre of the circle and then every second or third loop as the circle progresses.

Do not use pearl purl for items that you wish to use on a fairly frequent basis or that may catch on your clothes. Pearl purl is also awkward for items that need dusting! However, fine and very fine pearl purl can be used in some jewellery that is not handled frequently, such as earrings (see the Byzantine Empress Earrings, Project 11).

Couching smooth or rough purl

Lengths of smooth or rough purl are cut onto a piece of velvet-covered cardboard, and are sewn into position with couching thread that is threaded through one end of the hollow wire and secured at the other end. Smooth or rough purl can be laid straight over an area that needs filling (see the Medieval Palace Goldwork Sampler, Project 1). It can also be laid diagonally (see the Eighteenth-century French Flower Picture, Project 12) or in loops to form shapes (see the Elizabethan Heart-shaped Miniature Cushion, Project 2) or petals (see the Monsoon Wedding Paisley Gift Bag, Project 13).

Couching bright check

Small pieces of bright check are usually used to fill a space (see the Medieval Palace Goldwork Sampler, Project 1), and are sewn onto the background fabric like beads. Using scissors that you keep especially for cutting gold thread and wire, cut random lengths of bright check, ranging from 1–2 mm ($\frac{1}{24}$ – $\frac{1}{12}$ inch) in length. These pieces are then stitched in an ad hoc fashion over the entire space to be filled. As you build up the number of bright check pieces stitched within the area, a shimmering surface of gold will emerge.

T I P

As the designs may be enlarged or reduced according to your taste, no estimates have been given

for the amount of gold thread required as the length will vary according to the size of the design.

One method of working out the length of each gold thread required is to lay a piece of string or a

thin flexible fabric tape along the relevant design lines or within the relevant shape, remembering to

include another 2.5 cm (1 inch) each time you need to sink an end or start a new line.

Always err on the side of generosity.

Finishing your work

Once you have finished your design, you will need to remove your work from the frame.

However, before you do, check that the threads at the back of your work are all neatly couched down. Sometimes you will need to have done this during the creation of your work so that the back threads do not get in the way. It is a good job to do at the end of each goldwork session or when you feel like having a break from couching.

One of the easiest ways to tidy the back of your goldwork is to cut down the trailing threads to about 1.5 cm (½ inch) and thin out the extra gold of your Jap and twist threads. This is done by gently pulling on the twirl of gold around the central fibre core of each thread so that it is stretched out. Cut this piece of gold to about the same length as the fibrous part of the thread and overstitch the thread or threads (in a small, flat bundle) along the back of a couched line, perhaps with the thread you used for tacking your design.

When you are satisfied with the front and back of your work, take the time to steam the fabric before removing it from the frame. Steaming is very easy to do. Set your iron to the steam function and position the frame on the edge of your ironing board, with the back facing up. Position the iron about 2.5 cm (1 inch) above the work and allow the steam to penetrate the fabric below with steam for up to ten seconds. Repeat this procedure until every section of the back of your work has been steamed.

Some goldwork experts are not keen on this step. Your iron must not leak water when steaming, as drops can stain the fabric. However, if you have a reliable iron try steaming and see whether it makes a difference to the final look of your work. I certainly feel that it makes a difference to mine.

Leave the work in the frame overnight.

The next day, remove the fabric from the frame and make up the piece as instructed. For freestanding designs — those that will not be framed under glass — use acid-free cardboard to help define the shape of your work. When you have finished making your piece, you may wish to keep it wrapped in acid-free tissue paper when it is not in use or on display.

If you are framing your work, it is best to display your goldwork under glass, as the purls tend to tarnish if exposed directly to high humidity, sea breezes or heaters. Use a thick mount to make sure that the goldwork is not squashed against the glass. If the back of your work is heavily worked, you may wish to use a layer or two of light padding under the work so that it lies flat on a backboard (this is a board which is the size of the inside of your frame and onto which you will stretch your completed work).

Use acid-free cardboard for your backboard, and thick thread, such as quilting thread, to loop between the opposite edges of your work, stretching the work. Start in the middle of each edge and sew your thread between the top and bottom edges of the fabric, in a lacing pattern (you don't have to trim the calico away). Any ripples in the front of the work should be smoothed away. Next, work along the sides of the goldwork, tightening the edges of the fabric. You are now ready to insert your work into a frame.

Standard goldwork kit

If you are an embroiderer, you will most probably have most of the following equipment. Here is a useful checklist:

FRAMING-UP EQUIPMENT AND FABRIC

- Embroidery frame
- Frame 'tightener'
- Calico
- Background fabric (richly coloured silks, linen and velvet, as well as chiffon and other sheer fabrics, which can be laid over the base fabric to add interest)
- Soft acid-free tissue paper (for tracing patterns)
- Felt (dark yellow felt is particularly useful) for padding and for sewing into rolls onto which gold thread can be wound before use
- Kitchen twine (natural not synthetic, as synthetic twine stretches)

NEEDLES

- Needles for sewing kitchen twine around the frame and in calico
- Needles for stitching the background fabric onto the calico
- Needles with a narrow eye (such as sharps #11) for couching threads and for stab stitching padding
- Needles with a wide eye (such as Chenille needles #22) for sinking threads
- Needles with a wide eye (such as Chenille needles #18) for embroidery with gold Jacobean thread

THREADS

- Couching thread (silk and metallic)
- DMC stranded cotton for stitching fabric onto the calico (matching the colour of the fabric, if you so desire)
- Coloured silk threads for couching
- Cotton or polyester thread the same colour as the felt you are using (for dark yellow felt, you could use Mettler metrosene, No 100, colour 767)

SCISSORS

- A pair to cut your goldwork threads and wires
- A pair of embroidery scissors to cut couching and embroidery threads
- A pair to cut paper and felt

PINS AND THINGS

- Long dressmaker's pins with pearl ends
- Beeswax in a plastic container
- Flexible ruler with millimetres marked
- Piece of velvet-covered cardboard (see page 16)
- Tweezers
- Mellor (a silver goldworking tool that is pointed at one end and rounded at the other — used to help position gold threads)
- A pair of pliers to help pull kitchen twine through the calico

PROJECT 1
Medieval Palace Goldwork Sampler

T his project is an excellent way of honing your goldwork skills and techniques. The sampler has been designed to incorporate couched Jap gold and twist threads in straight lines and in circles, exploring how the thread works stitched on its own or massed. It uses a range of pearl purl, smooth purl, bright check, gold palettes and two types of gold beads to complete a shimmering sampler of gold.

YOU WILL NEED:

Standard goldwork kit (see page 20)

Special considerations for the background fabric:

Calico

Silks with a strong weave across the fabric (to help keep lines straight)

Felt (preferably dark yellow)

Couching thread:

Gold/yellow silk thread YLI #50 – 078

Stranded silk or cotton thread the same colour as your background fabric

Goldwork metal threads:

Jap gold (medium and thinner thread; here I used T70)

Gold twist (3 ply – a medium width)

Pearl purl (#2 – a medium width and a small amount of very fine pearl purl for the moon)

Smooth purl (#5 – medium width)

Bright check (#6 – medium width)

Jacobean thread

Beads and other decorations:

60 gold seed beads approximately 2 mm (1/12 inch) wide or you could try Mill Hill 00557

8 gold oval beads approximately 5 mm (1/4 inch) wide

60 gold palettes 3 mm (1/8 inch) wide

15 gold palettes approximately 1.8 mm (1/12 inch) long

Method

Frame up your calico and background fabric (see page 11), and trace the template for Project 1 onto some soft tracing paper. Once the background fabric is drum tight, transfer the design onto the fabric (see page 12). Cut out a template from a firm piece of paper for the five diamonds that will make up row 10. Attach the template to the felt using a pin or double-sided sticky tape. Using your sharp embroidery scissors, cut out the felt around the template. Repeat four more times. Put the five felt diamonds to one side.

The following instructions jump between rows. When working on a goldwork piece that requires a variety of different types of beads, palettes, goldwork threads and wires, it is important that you first work on rows that do not catch the thread. This is why we will first focus on couching Jap and twist threads, and leaving pearl purl, smooth purl, bright check and beads for last.

Row 1 (the bottom line of the design), couch a **single strand** of Jap gold thread in a straight line and sink the ends (see page 13).

Row 2, couch a **double strand** of Jap gold in a straight line and sink the ends. You will sew down the beads between rows 1 and 2 later on.

Row 4, couch a **double strand** of Jap gold and sink the ends.

Rows 6 and 8, couch a **double strand** of gold twist on each line and sink the ends.

Row 12, couch a **single strand** of gold twist and sink the end.

Rows 14 and 16, couch a **double strand** of gold twist and sink the ends.

Rows 18 and 20 (top line of the design), couch a **double strand** of Jap gold and sink the ends.

Row 17, couch a **double strand** of Jap gold into five small circles (see page 16) and sink the ends.

Row 9, with a **single strand** of Jap gold create a band of scrolls across the width of the sampler. Your couching stitch may be more than 3 mm (⅛ inch) apart. Concentrate on couching the top and bottom of each loop. Sink the ends.

Now tidy up the ends of gold threads on the underside of your fabric (see page 19).

Row 10, stab stitch (see box, page 54) the felt diamonds in a row. Position your first diamond in the middle of the row, stab stitching the felt into place. Stab stitch the other four diamonds in the row. Leave this row for now.

Row 11 is a simple example of Or Nue, a technique of building up a picture against rows of gold thread, using a coloured couching thread to delineate shapes. The sampler in the photograph uses fine strands of Jap (in particular T70) but you may use T71 or another fine Jap gold. Couch your first line of a **double strand** of Jap gold using the yellow silk thread for the walls spaced about 3 mm (⅛ inch) apart, as usual.

Now couch the same line with your coloured couching thread, starting with two couching stitches side by side to define the design line of the first tower. In the doorways, sew a number of couching stitches close together with your coloured thread so that you will eventually delineate doors, windows and rooflines. For the battlements, couch one strand of gold thread.

To achieve rounded or slanted edges, you can slant your couching stitches. For the battlements, couch a **single strand** of gold thread with a block of coloured couching stitches spaced at regular intervals — say

2 mm (1⁄12 inch). Abut the next **single strand** of gold thread above the first and stitch a block of coloured couching stitches in between the previous block of coloured stitches. This will give a chequered effect.

You will need to sink the ends of the gold threads progressively as you work up the design. You will soon be ready to tackle your first tower. It is advisable, after finishing the first tower, to sink the ends and tidy the threads of the entire Or Nue segment on the back of your work. For each tower, sink the ends (holding down the thread as you do so, so that you don't lose your short line of gold thread) and tidy them at the back of the work. This prevents your couching thread from getting caught up in the unsecured ends of gold thread. You will be coming back to this row later on.

Row 5, sew down a row of gold palettes. Secure your first palette with a stitch taken up through the middle of the palette and brought down to one side at the edge of the palette. The stitch should be parallel with the couched strands of gold thread on either side of the row. Position your next palette so that it overlaps the first and the securing stitch can be easily taken up through the middle of the second palette and brought down into the middle of the first. Build up a horizontal row of palettes. The securing stitches should appear to be a running stitch lying parallel to the couched threads.

Row 13, couch a slightly stretched strand of pearl purl to delineate three diamond shapes for this row. Using Jacobean thread, weave a raised stem band (see page 10) within each diamond shape.

Row 12, couch a slightly stretched out a row of pearl purl above the **single strand** of gold twist.

Row 11, couch a slightly stretched row of pearl purl around the silhouette of the entire fortress. Stretch out the very fine pearl purl and couch down two small curved pieces into the shape of the moon.

Row 10, couch pearl purl (slightly stretched out) around each of the five diamonds, hiding the edge of the felt. Fill the first, third and fifth diamonds with small pieces of bright check (see page 9). Cut about 30 small pieces of bright check and set aside so that you can use them for your starry sky in row 11 and a series of palettes and bright check in row 3.

For the second and fourth diamonds in row 10, lay pieces of smooth purl horizontally (see page 17) across the diamond, starting at the widest point in the middle of the diamond and varying the length as you progress towards the top and then the bottom of the shape.

Between rows 1 and 2, and for rows 7, 15 and 19, sew gold beads at regular intervals, 3 – 4 mm (1⁄8–1⁄6 inch) apart (see page 26).

Row 3, sew a row of single 3 mm (1⁄8 inch) palettes secured to the fabric with a small segment of bright check.

Row 11, complete the starry night with a scattering of 1.8 mm (approximately 1⁄12 inch) palettes secured to the fabric with a small segment of bright check.

For tips about finishing your work, see page 19.

Here is a tip for framing this work. As the threads on the underside of the work can be quite bulky around Row 11 (the Or Nue segment), it might be an idea to mount the work onto an acid-free frame of cardboard with a polystyrene core, which has a segment cut out in the middle.

PROJECT 2
Elizabethan Heart-shaped Miniature Cushion

This padded heart is designed to have a Elizabethan 'May-Day' atmosphere, enhanced by the use of a lattice of beautiful hand-dyed ribbon and rococo (crimped) gold thread. The repeated pattern in the middle of each diamond is a simple use of smooth and rough purl decorated with gold and coloured beads.

YOU WILL NEED:

Standard goldwork kit (see page 20), including the velvet-covered cardboard.

Other equipment:
A fabric marker
A piece of fairly stiff acid-free cardboard
Thin wadding either cotton or polyester
Strong cotton, matching the colour of the background fabric
Masking tape
PVA glue

Special considerations for the background fabric:
Calico
Shot silks or overlay your base silk with a lighter-textured fabric so that a two-tone shimmer occurs over the padded surface of the heart

Felt that matches the colour of the background fabric

Couching thread:
Gold/yellow silk thread YLI #50 – 078
Goldwork metal threads:
Rococo gold thread (medium weight)
Smooth purl (#5 – a medium width)
Rough purl (#5 – a medium width)

Beads and other decorations:
Hand-dyed variegated ribbon about 8 mm (¼ inch) diameter
60 gold seed beads approximately 2 mm (1/12 inch) diameter or you could try Mill Hill 00557
70 coloured beads matching your hand-dyed ribbon

Method

Frame up your calico and background fabric (see page 11) and trace the template for Project 2 onto some soft tracing paper. Once the background fabric is drum tight on its frame, transfer the design onto the fabric (see page 12).

Weave a lattice of the ribbon across the heart, leaving each strand of ribbon 2.5 cm (1 inch) beyond the outline of the heart. You may secure the ribbon temporarily with one or two tiny stitches at the end of each strand beyond the outline of the heart.

Couch down **single strands** of rococo gold thread along the middle of each ribbon lying from the top left to the bottom right of the heart. Position a couching stitch in each valley of the crimped gold thread. Then couch rococo gold threads over the lines of the ribbon lattice that run diagonally from the top right to the bottom left.

You may then start the simple pattern of smooth purl in the three middle cells of the heart, starting with the top cell. Mark a small circle in the middle of the cell with your fabric marker.

Each cell needs 4 lengths of smooth purl measuring 1 cm (⅜ inch) and 4 lengths of rough purl measuring 5 mm (¼ inch).

To the left of the upper point of the small circle, bring your needle of couching thread up through the fabric and thread the 1 cm (⅜ inch) length of smooth purl onto the needle. Bring the needle down 2 mm (½ inch) from the first point, forming a petal. Pull the thread lightly so that you don't contract the smooth purl tubing. Position a couching stitch at the upper loop of your purl. Bring your needle up near the right-hand end of the first petal. Again thread a 1 cm (⅜ inch) length of smooth purl onto the needle and form another petal, securing the top of the loop with a couching stitch. Do this twice more so that you have a four-petal flower.

In the middle of each petal, bring up the needle of couching thread through the fabric and thread the 5 mm (¼ inch) length of rough purl. Bring the needle down beyond the top loop along the middle of the petal, hiding the petal's couching stitch. Do this for every petal.

With a double strand of couching thread, sew a coloured bead in the middle of the four petals and in each corner of the cell (see box, below). Sew a gold bead in between each petal.

Repeat this pattern in each cell of the lattice, omitting some of the beads at the very edge of the heart.

When you have finished your work, see page 19 for removing the work from your frame.

Cut the excess fabric and calico from about 2.5 cm (1 in) around the outline of the heart. Cut out a heart shape from the cardboard. Also cut out four heart-shaped pieces of decreasing

---

Instructions for sewing single beads onto fabric

Use a double strand of couching thread with a knot at the end. Bring your needle up at the point where you would like your bead to sit. Thread your bead and bring the needle down close to where it first emerged. Bring your needle up again at right angles to the first securing stitch, and then bring the needle down on the other side of the bead, making sure that the double thread subdivides on either side of the bead as the thread is pulled through the fabric. This stitch, resembling a cross-stitch, will secure the bead so that it sits well on the fabric.

size from the wadding. Place the four pieces of wadding in decreasing size on the cardboard heart and secure each layer with double-sided sticky tape. Position the goldwork heart over the top and flip over.

Carefully clip the exposed excess fabric so that the edges will fold smoothly over the edge of the cardboard. Using a long length of strong cotton with a knot tied at one end, bring the needle up through the flaps at the top left of the heart and then bring the needle up through the flaps at the bottom right of the heart, pulling

the flaps as close together as the fabric allows. Continue working around the heart, bringing all the flaps close together into the centre of the piece. Check your work frequently to ensure that the pattern is well positioned on the front of the heart.

Fold a piece of rococo thread and position a loop from the top centre of the heart on the back of the cardboard. Secure it with masking tape. Cut the felt so that it is the same size as the cardboard heart. Carefully use PVA glue to secure the felt onto the back of the heart.

PROJECT 3
Japanese-style Damascened Needle Case

This useful case catches the light quite beautifully and requires only one type of goldwork thread for its decoration. The design owes something to the work of Gustav Klimt (1862–1918) who was keen on the use of circles, rectangles and other repeated geometric designs as background texture in his paintings.

YOU WILL NEED:

Standard goldwork kit (see page 20)

Special considerations for the background fabric:

   Calico

   A light, delicately coloured silk

   Thin felt matching the colour of the background silk

Other equipment:

   A fabric marker

   Two pieces of stiff acid-free cardboard measuring 8 cm (3⅛ inches) by 11 cm (4¼ inches)

A piece of thin wadding, measuring 8 cm (3⅛ inches) by 11 cm (4¼ inches)

Masking tape

PVA glue or spray adhesive

Couching thread:

   Gold/yellow silk thread YLI #50 – 078

   Goldwork metal threads:

   Jap gold (T71)

   Gold twist (3 ply – a medium width)

   Gold twist (2 by 2 – a thick width)

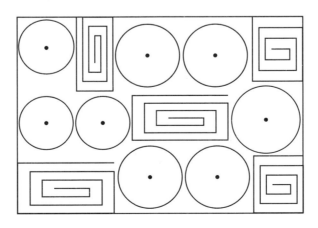

Method

Frame up your calico and background fabric (see page 11). Enlarge the template to 7 cm (2 ¾ inches) x 10 cm (4 inches) and trace the design onto some soft tracing paper. Once the fabric is drum tight, transfer the design onto your background fabric (see page 12).

The main design is made up of three segments, all using the same gold thread and couching thread. Tackle the rectangles first. Using a **double strand** of gold thread, start working on the outline of one of the rectangles. If you are confident with couching, start on the rectangle in the middle. If you are using this as a practice piece, start on a rectangle in the corner.

For each rectangle, outline the shape first and then start filling the interior with row upon row of couched lines. This will provide an excellent opportunity for you to become familiar with turning corners (see page 16) with gold thread. As you progress towards the middle, there will soon be very little space to turn. At this point, end the filling by making one final tight turn and couching a final line across the length of the remaining space. Try not to leave any space showing. Sink all the ends and tidy up the threads at the back of the work.

The second part of the design is the working of the circles. This time you will be starting your couching from the centre of each circle (see page 16). Continue couching a **double strand** of gold thread until the circle is large enough to hit either one of the rectangles or the outer edge of the design. Sink all the ends and tidy up the threads at the back of the work.

The third part to completing this design is the couching of a **single strand** of gold thread in the shapes left between the rectangles, circles and the outer edge of the design. The thinner the gold thread, the easier this part of the project will be.

Manipulate the gold thread in tight spirals around the outer edges of the circles, keeping the thread strictly within the border of the design. It is advisable when filling spaces around the rectangle to avoid tight spirals and instead to do a series of tight loops positioned diagonally to the rectangle (this ensures that you don't inadvertently extend the shape of the rectangle).

Once you have finished all your couching, stitch a length of 3 ply gold twist around the border, starting in the bottom left-hand corner.

On one piece of stiff cardboard, place the wadding and then overlay it with your design. Use masking tape or cotton to frame your work tightly over the edges of the cardboard, making sure that the border of the design stays straight and at equal distance from the edge of the cardboard. Over the other piece of cardboard, frame up some of the spare background fabric without any wadding.

Hold the two pieces of covered cardboard so that the back of both panels is on the inside. Take the thick twist and, holding the two panels on their side, couch the twist along the edge making sure that the thread picks up a bit of fabric from the front and back panel while at the same time encircling the thick gold thread. This is going to be the hinge for your needle case. As thick twist easily frays, start the couching with ten or so tiny couching stitches bunched up tidily at the beginning of the twist and end the same way.

Open your little book and, on the inside of the panels, paste (using either PVA Glue or a spray adhesive sprayed only on the back of the felt) two rectangles of felt cut slightly smaller than the cardboard.

You now have a beautiful needle case for yourself or a precious gift for a dear friend.

PROJECT 4
Art Nouveau Hair Clip

This delightful hair clip is inspired by the jewellery designs of the French Art Nouveau designer Georges Fouquet (1862–1957). It is a relatively simple goldwork project that can be couched against a rich silk fabric, preferably of shot silk that shimmers against your hair.

YOU WILL NEED:

Standard goldwork kit (see page 20)

Special considerations for the background fabric:

Calico

Shot silks that provide a contrast to your hair colour or that match a favourite outfit

Felt matching the background silk fabric (cut out in the shape of the hair clip template)

Other equipment:

A piece of acid-free cardboard of medium stiffness cut out in the shape of the hair clip template

A piece of thin wadding, cut to the same size as the piece of cardboard

Hair clip (the metal clip only, without any decoration; available from bead or craft suppliers)

Masking tape

PVA glue or spray adhesive

Couching thread:

Gold/yellow silk thread YLI #50 – 078

Goldwork metal threads:

Gold twist (3 ply – a medium width)

Pearl purl (#1 – a fine width)

Beads and other decorations

60 gold seed beads approximately 2 mm ($\frac{1}{12}$ inch) diameter or you could try Mill Hill 00557

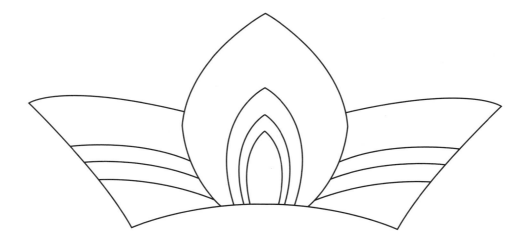

Method

Frame up your calico and background fabric (see page 11), and trace the template for Project 4 onto some soft tracing paper. Once the fabric is drum tight, transfer the design onto your background fabric (see page 12).

Start in the middle of the design. Pull apart about 12 cm (4¾ inches) of the pearl purl so that the loops are slightly separated (see page 17). Starting with the middle segment, outline the largest arch in the middle of the design. Couch it into place, sewing couching stitches every two or three loops and two couching stitches at the very apex of the arch. Couch down the other side of the arch and end by cutting the bottom of the wire loop where the design line ends.

Couch down the next inner arch in the middle of the design. Then couch down a line of pearl purl from the final two inner curved lines in the very middle of the design.

Using a **single strand** of gold twist, couch down the loops of gold twist within the outer two arches of pearl purl. Start the gold twist slightly above the design line with two

couching stitches, manipulating the thread into larger loops as you progress to the top of the arch. Do the same on the other side. Sink the ends of the gold twist so that the thread ends neatly near the end of the inner arch of pearl purl. Make sure that you have the same number of loops on each side.

On the right and left 'wings' of the design, couch down three slightly curved, parallel lines of pearl purl. Above the top and bottom lines again couch loops of gold twist. Sink the ends so that they disappear, neatly abutting a pearl purl line or the outline of the design.

Sew gold beads in the fullest part of each loop so that the beads appear to be alternating on the right and left side of the design. You may decide, as we have done, not to sew gold beads in the lower right and left wings of the design. However, you will do well to sew gold beads within the two most inner arches in the middle of the design.

When you have finished your work, follow the instructions on page 19 for removing the work from your frame.

Cut the excess fabric and calico from about 2.5 cm (1 inch) around the outline of the hair clip. Place the pre-cut wadding over the cardboard backing, position the goldwork design over the top and flip it over. Carefully clip the exposed excess fabric so that the flaps fold smoothly over the edge of the cardboard. Using small lengths of masking tape, catch down the flaps of the fabric over the edge of the cardboard and stick them to the back of the cardboard, folding the fabric neatly at the corners.

Once satisfied with the position of the design over the cardboard background, gently flex the cardboard so that its curve matches that of the metal hair clip. Check your felt piece to make sure that it is slightly smaller than the cardboard shape and, using PVA or spray adhesive (sprayed onto the felt rather than the goldwork), stick the felt to the back of the cardboard. Use the PVA to attach the clip to the middle of the felt back. Allow the hair clip to dry (following the manufacturer's recommendations).

If giving the hair clip as a gift, you could present it in a pretty brown box packed with lots of tissue paper.

Project 1 – Medieval Palace Goldwork Sampler

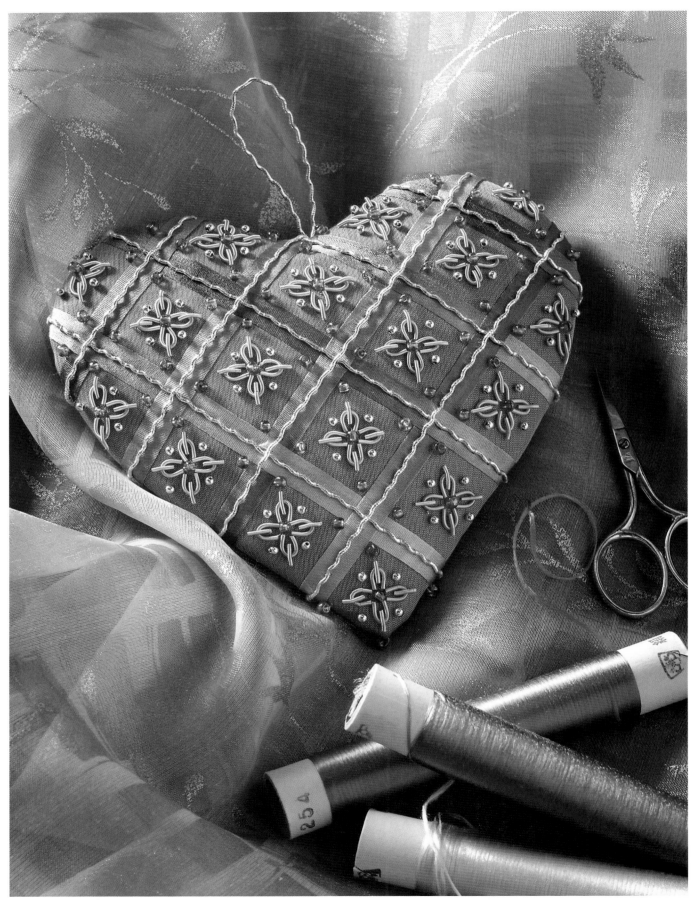

Project 2 – Elizabethan Heart-shaped Miniature Cushion

Project 4 – Art Nouveau Hair Clip

Project 5 – Renaissance Velvet Wrap Trim

Project 3 – Japanese-style Damascened Needle Case

Project 6 – Belle Epoch Notebook Cover

Project 7 – Ancient Egyptian Ornament Nine-square Grid Pattern

Project 8 – Dream of Summer Butterflies Tea Light Lampshade

Project 15 – Merry Yule Christmas Ornaments

Project 11 – Byzantine Empress Goldwork Earrings

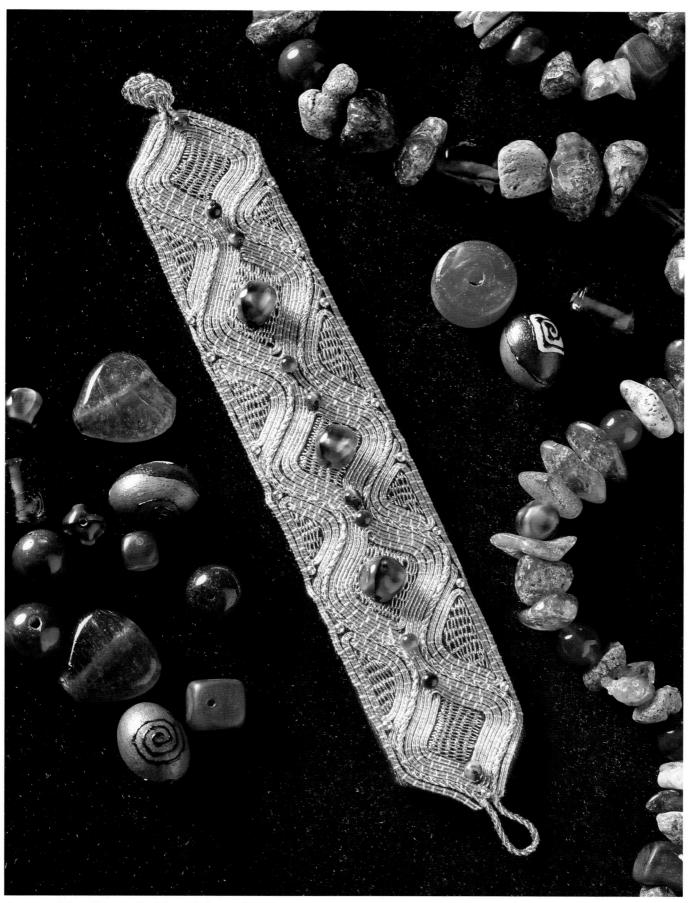

Project 10 – Ethnic Goldwork Bracelet

Project 9 – Folk Art Goldwork Frame

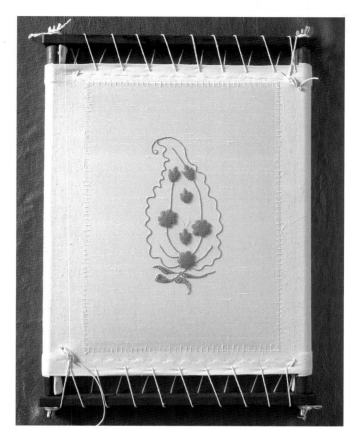

Above left: The Monsoon
Wedding Paisley Motif
shown as a work in progress
on the embroidery frame

Above right: Project 13 –
Monsoon Wedding Paisley
Motif Wedding Gift Bag

Left: Project 12 – Eighteenth-
century French Flower
Picture

Project 14 – Eclectic Goldwork Handbag

PROJECT 5
Renaissance Velvet Wrap Trim

The beauty, variety and ingenuity of Renaissance lace are the inspiration for the design of this work. This design is specially adapted to goldwork so that a single line can be couched around a substantial portion of the central motif without the need to sink too many ends. As an edging for a velvet wrap, this work will help you develop your couching skills as you manoeuvre single strands of silver twist into flowers, urns and scrolls.

YOU WILL NEED:

Standard goldwork kit (see page 20)

Special considerations for the background fabric:

Dark or richly coloured velvet

Satin backing fabric

Couching thread:

Silver metallic thread (I used Metallic Madeira No 40, silver or equivalent)

Black cotton or polyester thread for sewing the garment together and to bead the tassels (optional)

Goldwork metal threads:

Silver twist (3 ply – a medium width)

Thick silver twist (possibly 2 x 2)

Beads and other decorations:

Pearl beads approximately 4 mm (⅙ inch) diameter

Pearl beads approximately 2 mm (¹⁄₁₂ inch) diameter

Silver palettes 3 mm (⅛ inch) or 1.8 mm (approximately ¹⁄₁₂ inch) long

Silver seed beads

6 black tassels (if making a wide wrap with three arches on each edge of the wrap)

Method

Frame up your velvet without any calico (see page 11), and trace the template for Project 5 onto some soft tracing paper. If you wish to make a wide wrap, copy three of the templates. If you want to make a narrow scarf, use only one template at each end. Once the fabric is drum tight, transfer the design onto your background fabric (see page 12). Alternatively, you may consider sewing the design onto a silk fabric that can then be appliquéd onto the velvet wrap.

When you are satisfied with the design, sew a **single strand** of the thick silver twist along the upper and lower line of the large band connecting the three arches (if you are making a wide wrap). Do not sink this twist but capture each end with a couple of couching stitches. Extend this line beyond the line of the design so that when the lining is added the ends of the thick silver twist will be caught within the lining.

Couch the thinner silver twist on the two inner lines of the wide band, outline the main two lines of the arches with the thinner silver twist, and then work on the inner design within each arch.

Decorate the outer edge of each arch with a continuous flow of ogee shapes, couched with a single strand of silver twist.

TIP

When you have a complex design to couch, thread up three or four needles with couching thread, remembering to tie a knot at the end. This will reduce the time you spend between couching.

Within each flower in the central panel design, sew a 4 mm (⅙ inch) pearl bead in the centre.

Sew 4 mm (⅙ inch) pearl beads at regular intervals within the two narrow bands of the wide band and 2 mm (½₂ inch) pearl beads at regular intervals within the two lines of each arch. In the middle of each ogee shape along the side of each arch, sew a silver palette secured with a silver bead. Sew a silver bugle bead between each ogee shape.

Repeat these instructions for the other edge of the wrap, carefully rolling the completed edge within some acid-free tissue paper onto your frame and framing-up as usual the other end of the wrap.

When you have finished your work, follow the instructions on page 19 for removing the work from your frame.

Cut excess fabric to about 2.5 cm (1 inch) beyond the ogee-lined arches. Cut the lining to follow the same shape as the velvet and attach the lining to the velvet, leaving a space at the apex of each arch so that a tassel can be threaded through and secured between the velvet and the satin backing. Leave a length of fabric in the middle of the wrap where the lining is not attached to the velvet, and clip the fabric along the edges where the arches curve. Opening the wrap along the unsewn side, thread a tassel through for each arch so that the tassels are nestling between the fabric and backing. Sew the tail of each tassel firmly to the tip of its arch with black thread.

Turn the wrap inside out and shake out the arches so that each arch is filled out and the tassel is swinging freely. You may wish to decorate your tassel with any left-over pearl or silver beads. Carefully sew them into the tassel with black cotton and thread the pearls so that they hang in swags around the tassel.

PROJECT 6
Belle Epoch Notebook Cover

The decorative motifs and fun of the Belle Epoch, at the turn of the twentieth century, is captured in this delightful notebook cover. The swirls and stripes characteristic of this era are completed by a ruffle of ribbon that echoes the skirt ruffles of the dancing girls so beloved of Toulouse Lautrec (1864–1901).

YOU WILL NEED:

Standard goldwork kit (see page 20)

Special considerations for the background fabric:
  Calico
  Sturdy silks with a strong weave

Other equipment:
  A plain notebook of size and dimensions to suit the template design
  A stiff thin piece of acid-free cardboard (optional, if making simply the front cover)
  Thin wadding, cut the same size as the front cover of the notebook
  Masking tape
  PVA glue or spray adhesive

Threads:
  Gold/yellow silk thread YLI #50 – 078
  Hand-dyed silk threads that contrast with and enhance the colour of the background fabric

Goldwork metal threads:
  Gold twist (3 ply – a medium width)
  A thick gold twist (optional, for couching around the edges of the work if used as the front cover of the notebook)
  Pearl purl (#2 – a medium width)

Beads and other decorations:
  300 gold seed beads approximately 2 mm ($\frac{1}{12}$ inch) diameter or you could try Mill Hill 00557
  A small selection of 4 mm ($\frac{1}{6}$ inch) gold round beads
  A length of chain, approximately 3 mm ($\frac{1}{8}$ inch) wide
  Ribbon 2.5 cm (1 inch) wide in a colour that matches or contrasts with your chosen background fabric
  Seed beads that match the colour of your ribbon

Method

Frame up your calico and background fabric (see page 11), and trace the template for Project 6 onto some soft tracing paper. Adjust the size of the design to suit the shape of your notebook. When the fabric on the frame is drum tight, transfer the design onto your background fabric (see page 12). You may decide to cover the whole book with the fabric, or if the book's existing cover matches your fabric, you could simply attach the design as a front panel to the existing book cover. If you have no experience with covering notebooks, you might wish to ask a professional bookbinder to help you.

To get used to couching twist, work on the scroll design using a **single strand** of gold twist. If you feel confident, couch a **double strand**, consisting of your gold thread and a strand of hand-dyed silk. Sink the ends and tidy up the back.

Using a **double strand** of gold twist, couch the two curved horizontal lines above the scroll and the line below the scrolled section. Also couch the two outermost long vertical lines running all the way from the top to the bottom of the design with two strands of gold twist.

To achieve the striped effect in the upper part of the work, couch a double strand consisting of a single strand of gold twist and a strand of hand-dyed silk thread. In between every second stripe, sew a length of chain, attaching the chain with couching thread through the link of each chain.

Under the second curved horizontal line, sew down another length of chain. Under the chain, sew a row of beads the colour of which matches the ribbon that you will soon be attaching to the design. Sew another row of coloured beads above the curved line under the scrolled segment.

To achieve the striped effect in the lower part of the design, bead straight lengths of gold seed beads. In between every second line, couch a line of pearl purl (which has been slightly pulled apart (see page 17)).

With a coloured cotton or polyester thread that matches your ribbon, sew wide stitches along the ribbon in a zigzag pattern, pulling the thread through the ribbon so that it ruches. Attach the ruched ribbon to the goldwork

---

To attach a long chain of seed beads

Bring a needle and thread up at the point where you want your beaded line to start. Thread all the beads you need to outline a particular design line (leaving off one or two beads, as they tend to spread out a little when couching thread is used in between each or every second bead). You can use a couching needle and thread for the beads or a specially designed (much longer) beading needle (for example, a Bohin Couture, No 10/12 Enfiler Les Perles Assorties).

With another couching needle and thread, sew a small couching stitch between the first and second bead, catching the thread holding the line of beads together. Couch between the second and third bead and then sew a couching stitch between every second or third bead. Continue until the second last bead in the line. Tie off the thread you have been using to couch down the beads and finish the last bead by sewing the thread that has been holding the beads together into the back of the fabric.

design so that it sits between the vertical lines of the design. Attach a scattering of gold beads over the ruched ribbon. Also, sew some gold beads in the centre of some of the scrolls.

When you have finished your work, follow the instructions on page 19 for removing the work from your frame.

Cut the excess calico within a few millimetres (about ⅛ inch) of the couched vertical lines.

Stretch your fabric over the cardboard and wadding. Use masking tape or cotton to secure the fabric and wadding. Glue the cover onto the existing cover of the book and consider edging the new cover with thick gold twist, beginning and ending in the bottom left-hand corner. Or seek advice from a professional bookbinder as to how to cover the entire notebook with the fabric.

PROJECT 7
Ancient Egyptian Ornament Nine-square Grid Pattern

This design is adapted from an interesting colour plate of ancient Egyptian decorative motifs from *The Grammar of Ornament*, an English publication produced in 1856. It contains colour plates of decorative motifs from various eras and cultures compiled by Owen Jones (1809–1874). This book, which is still in print, is an excellent source of inspiration for goldworkers and embroiderers alike.

The ancient Egyptian ornament chosen as an unusual illustration of the nine-square grid pattern involves couching colour twists in spirals and as loops forming ten-petal flowers. Turn this into a miniature wall hanging or frame the design with fabric, to evoke the mysteries of ancient Egypt.

YOU WILL NEED:

Standard goldwork kit (see page 20)

Special considerations for the background fabric:

Calico

A gold-coloured background fabric that can be matched with layers of turquoise, red and green coloured silks

Couching thread:

Gold/yellow silk thread YLI #50 – 078

Goldwork metal threads:

Gold Jap

Coloured twist (medium width), preferably blue, green and red. For a more vivid effect, try a combination of DMC metallic threads, including red (5270), blue (5290) and green (5269)

Red or terracotta coloured rough purl

Beads and other decorations:

Nine round gold beads approximately 4 mm (⅙ inch)

Nine 8 mm (⅓ inch) gold palettes

Method

Frame up your calico and background fabric (see page 11), and trace the template for Project 7 (enlarge if you wish) onto some soft tracing paper. Once the fabric on the frame is drum tight, transfer the design onto your background fabric (see page 12).

Sew a palette in the middle of each spiral or flower and secure it with a gold bead. Start in the middle of the design. Start couching one spiral around the palette with a **double strand** of Jap gold and metallic green thread. Before completing a full circuit of the gold and green combination, start a new **double strand** of Jap gold and metallic red thread. Couch this new strand with another needle threaded with couching thread. Continue couching the gold and green strands, alternating with the gold and red strands.

Alternatively, you can couch a spiral of Jap gold and green, leaving space to couch the spiral of Jap gold and red once you have finished the entire circle. Continue couching the gold and green line towards the edge of the design into another spiral. Couch the gold and red line along another design line so that it flows into a different spiral.

For each flower, use a **double strand** of Jap gold and blue twist, turning corners tightly against the sequin in the middle to make tight loops of ten petals. Cut a length of red rough purl approximately 5 mm (¼ inch) and sew it lengthwise in the middle of each of the petals.

When you have finished your work, follow the instructions on page 19 for removing the work from your frame.

Cut a panel from a stiff piece of acid-free cardboard so that, when the goldwork is mounted on the cardboard, a border of undecorated silk exists between the design and the edge. Mount this board on top of a combined layer of turquoise, gold and red fabrics. Frame or mount the entire work on a backboard that can be hung directly against a wall.

PROJECT 8
Dream of Summer
Butterflies Tea Light Lampshade

This deliciously summery lampshade evokes a charming Russian air with the use of pearl beads and a light filigree of fine gilt thread. When the candle is alight, the butterfly will shimmer as the light highlights the delicate pattern of its wings.

YOU WILL NEED:

Standard goldwork kit (see page 20)

Special considerations for the background fabric:

A fabric that shimmers with an interesting metallic lustre

Stiff white interfacing

Other equipment:

A piece of thin cardboard

A small lamp frame or tea light lamp frame

White satin bias binding

PVA glue and spray adhesive

Couching thread:

Gold/yellow silk thread YLI #50 – 078

Goldwork metal threads:

Gold twist (3 ply – a medium width)

Silver gold twist (3 ply – a medium width)

Fine passing thread (gilt, see page 10)

Beads and other decorations:

50 pearl beads approximately 4 mm (⅙ inch) plus extra if you want to edge your lampshade with beads

50 seed beads that match the colour of your background fabric

Method

Frame up your interfacing and background fabric (see page 11, but omit the calico; the interfacing will be sufficient), and trace the template (adjusting the size to suit your lampshade) for Project 8 onto some soft tracing paper. Place your lampshade frame on its side on a piece of thin cardboard. Roll the frame from strut to strut as you trace out the exact shape (top and bottom) needed to cover the frame. Cut out the shape and fit it around the frame, making any necessary adjustments. This is your initial lampshade template.

To check the best size and position of your butterfly, temporarily tape your initial lampshade template into the shape of the frame and position the butterfly template on it. When you are happy with how the lampshade will look, make another tracing of the lampshade template complete with your butterfly design. This is your final template.

Once the fabric on the frame is drum tight, transfer the final template (the complete design) onto your background fabric (see page 12), allowing for at least 1 cm (3⁄8 inch) beyond the top and bottom lines of the lampshade template and along one of the side edges.

To begin your goldwork, outline the wings with a **single strand** of gold twist. Also subdivide each wing into three segments as indicated on the design with a **single strand** of gold twist. Tidy the ends of the gold twist at the back of the work and sew them into the back of each couched line. Fill each middle segment of the four wings with a **single strand** of silver gold twist, filling each section as solidly as possible, and allowing the inevitable open corners to become a decorative feature in themselves. Outline the central body of the butterfly with a single strand of silver gold twist. Sink the ends and couch them down along the more solid areas of couched gold.

Using the thin passing thread, couch a line of fine passing thread in a zig-zag pattern around the filled central panels of silver gold twist. Do this for all four wings, couching the top and bottom of each loop. Using passing thread, sew the antennae of the butterfly, passing the gold thread through the fabric to make the 'V' shape.

Thread a row of alternating pearls and coloured seed beads and couch a row of beads along each edge of the butterfly's wings (see page 37). You may also wish to couch a row of beads in this same pattern onto a white satin bias binding that can be glued at the top and bottom edges of the lampshade when it is finished. Sew a pearl bead at the end of each antenna and above the body of the butterfly.

When you have finished your work, follow the instructions on page 19 for removing the work from your frame.

Cut the excess fabric and interfacing from about 1 cm (⅜ inch) around the top and bottom lines of the lampshade template and along one of the side edges. Spray adhesive onto the cardboard lampshade template and gently position the fabric over the sticky surface. Use PVA glue to turn and secure the edge along one of the sides. Clip the fabric above and below the top and bottom edges so that the fabric can be eased over the cardboard, securing each segment of fabric with PVA glue.

When dry, bend the fabric-covered lampshade template into the size required by the frame and glue the back edges together with one side (on which the fabric is neatly turned over) over the other (where the fabric would be flush with the edge of the template). Use PVA glue and hold the top and bottom edges together with plastic clothes pegs. As an optional extra, glue the beaded white satin bias binding along the inner top and bottom edges of the lampshade.

Match the finished lampshade with a delicate gold base.

PROJECT 9
Folk Art Goldwork Frame

Simple folk art decorative motifs can provide a source of inspiration for the goldwork designer. Here, simple spirals and a decorative motif known as Elizabethan loops make a charming frame, decorated with pearl beads.

YOU WILL NEED:

Standard goldwork kit (see page 20)

Special considerations for the background fabric:

Calico

Shot silks or a gold silk covered with a shot chiffon fabric so that interesting hue changes occur when the frame is padded

Other equipment:

Two pieces of stiff acid-free cardboard, one cut in the shape of the frame template and the other cut to form the rectangular backing to the frame

Four layers of wadding, cut in the same shape as the frame template (but in diminishing sizes)

A cardboard or plywood backing with a hinged strut that can move to support the upright frame

Framer's masking tape

Double-sided sticky tape

PVA glue

Couching thread:

Gold/yellow silk thread YLI #50 – 078

Goldwork metal threads:

Gold twist (3 ply – a medium width)

Thick twist (2 x 2 or 3 x 3)

Beads and other decorations:

36 pearl ellipsoid beads approximately 6 mm (¼ inch) wide

Method

Frame up your calico and background fabric (see page 11), and trace the template for Project 9 (enlarge if you wish) onto some soft tracing paper. Once the fabric on the frame is drum tight, transfer the design onto your background fabric (see page 12).

Start by couching a **single strand** of the thick twist around the outer and inner outlines of the frame. As you cannot sink these ends without damaging your fabric, start couching the thick twist in the bottom left-hand corner by sewing half a dozen couching stitches to secure the thread and stop it from fraying. End the couching of the thick twist by cutting the twist cleanly and quickly (before it starts to fray again!) sewing a number of couching stitches over the end to secure it.

Turn to the top of the frame design and start couching a double strand of the medium width twist into a double spiral. Start from the middle of the left-hand spiral, leaving an equal distance between the emerging circles of gold twist and end in the middle of the right-hand spiral. When you have finished, couch the double spiral pattern at the bottom of the frame design.

Next, work on the Elizabethan loops on the bottom left-hand side of the frame, making sure that each loop is large enough to comfortably surround your ellipsoidal pearl beads. Continue couching the twist up the frame into a single spiral, ending in the middle of the spiral. Start the twist again (leaving a tail end of 2.5 cm (1 inch), which you will sink and tidy up at the back) above the spiral, and continue the pattern up the left-hand side of the frame.

Work on the right-hand side of the frame in the same manner. Sew the ellipsoidal pearl beads within each gold loop all around the frame.

When you have finished your work, follow the instructions on page 19 for removing the work from your frame.

Cut the excess fabric and calico from about 2.5 cm (1 inch) around the outline of the frame.

Place the prepared layers of wadding over the cardboard, with the largest piece of wadding against the cardboard and the smaller pieces stacked up to the smallest layer. Use double-sided sticky tape between each layer. Position the goldwork design over the top and flip the piece over. Carefully cut a cross in the inner rectangle of the frame so that the flaps of the frame can be secured around the inner edges of the cardboard frame. Trim the inner flaps and secure them at the back of the frame with masking tape. Try to keep the thick twist edging straight and in position around the edge of the inner part of the frame.

Stretch the outer edges of the goldwork fabric around the edge of the cardboard and secure them with masking tape, folding the fabric neatly at the corners.

Once satisfied with the position of the design over the cardboard background, cover the backing cardboard with a piece of the background fabric, securing the fabric over the edge of the cardboard with masking tape. To secure the backing to the frame, couch the thick twist along the sides and bottom of the frame so that the twist sits along the edge of the backing. This will leave the top free so that you can slide your picture into the frame. Glue the backing with a hinged strut to the back of the frame covering the masking tape securing the fabric, and making sure that the strut adequately supports the frame.

Slide a photograph through the slot at the top.

PROJECT 10
Ethnic Goldwork Bracelet

A dramatically beautiful goldwork bracelet that is easy to make and light to wear. Woven goldwork punctuates an ethnic-style design where strands of gold Jap and twist lazily flow around islands of woven gold surmounted with organically shaped beads and scatterings of gold seed beads and shimmering beads of yellow and black tiger's eye.

YOU WILL NEED:

Standard goldwork kit (see page 20)

Special considerations for the background fabric:
Calico
Stiff black interfacing
Black grosgrain ribbon 2.5 cm (1 inch) wide

Couching thread:
Gold/yellow silk thread YLI #50 – 078

Goldwork metal threads:
Thick gold twist (2 x 2 – a thick width)
Jap gold (medium width)
Jacobean thread

Beads and other decorations:
18 gold seed beads approximately 2 mm ($\frac{1}{12}$ inch) diameter or you could try Mill Hill 00557
3 organically shaped beads
10 tiger's eye beads approximately 4 mm ($\frac{1}{6}$ inch) diameter

Method

Frame up your calico and black interfacing (see page 11), and trace the template for Project 10 onto some soft tracing paper. Make sure that the interfacing is 2.5 cm (1 inch) wider and longer than the actual design. Once the fabric on the frame is drum-tight, transfer the design onto the black interfacing (see page 12).

Start by couching the thick gold twist at one end of the bracelet design, leaving a tail of 7.5 cm (3 inches). Secure the thick twist at the beginning with six or seven couching stitches, and then couch the thick twist in an undulating pattern along the length of the design. When you reach the other end, again secure the thread with six or seven couching stitches and make a medium-sized loop that stands free of the background fabric.

Couch the twist onto the background fabric, couching the thread down so that the loop is secured. Continue couching the twist in an undulating line back to the beginning. When you returned to the point where you started couching the gold twist, secure the thread with a number of couching stitches and leave a tail of 7.5 cm (3 inches).

Five softened diamond shapes should have been formed along the line of the bracelet by the thick gold twist. Eight irregularly shaped triangular side panels should also have been created.

With a **double strand** of Jap gold, outline the shape of the length of the bracelet and then couch three rows of double strand Jap gold within the diamond shapes (on the inside of the gold twist) forming two rows of double strand Jap gold in the triangular side panels. This will leave you with five irregularly shaped squares and eight irregularly shaped triangles. These will be filled with a woven stitch based on the raised stem band (see page 10), worked with your gold Jacobean thread.

If you are confident with sewing a raised stem band stitch, rather than covering the entire surface of the middle three diamonds, you could sew a raised stem band that leaves some space in the middle of the square so that a large bead can sit comfortably against the gold decoration.

Sew gold beads on the outer edges of the bracelet where the turning of gold Jap has left some black interfacing showing through. A small gold bead can also be sewn at the point where the gold twist loop joins the background fabric. Sew the tiger's eye beads in an irregular row in the centre of the bracelet, one at each end and two between each gold woven diamond (in the spaces left by the corners of the couched Jap gold).

When you have finished your work, follow the instructions on page 19 for removing the work from your frame.

Cut the excess calico from around the outline of the bracelet, leaving the black interfacing. At each end on the back, fold the interfacing so that the edge is tucked away neatly. Sew down the flaps. Fold the long sides of the interfacing into the centre and sew down. Finish off by overstitching a length of grosgrain ribbon over the interfacing and making a knot in the gold twist threads left at one end of the bracelet. Using couching thread, sew tiny stitches to secure the knot, as it will otherwise unravel over time, or thread on a bead with a drilled hole through which the two threads can pass, securing the ends neatly.

PROJECT 11
Byzantine Empress Goldwork Earrings

Lightweight and jewel-like, the design of these goldwork earrings is based on Byzantine metalwork jewellery. Make several pairs in different colours to suit your wardrobe or to give to your friends as gifts.

YOU WILL NEED:

Standard goldwork kit (see page 20)

Special considerations for the background fabric:

Silk that matches a favourite outfit

Stiff interfacing

Thin felt matching the background silk fabric, cut in the shape of the earrings template

Other equipment:

Two pieces of acid-free cardboard of medium stiffness

Masking tape

PVA glue or spray adhesive

Two earring findings (especially those that end in a wire shaped as a circle)

Couching thread:

Gold/yellow silk thread YLI #50 – 078

Goldwork metal threads:

Pearl purl (#2 – medium width)

Pearl purl (very fine)

Jacobean thread or passing thread (No 4)

Beads and other decorations:

260 gold petite seed beads approximately 1 mm ($^1/_{24}$ inch) diameter or you could try Mill Hill 40557

Two round gold beads approximately 2 mm ($^1/_{12}$ inch) diameter

Method

Frame up your interfacing and background fabric (see page 11, but do not use calico; the interfacing will be sufficient), and trace the template for Project 11 onto some soft tracing paper. When the fabric on the frame is drum tight, transfer the design onto the interfacing (see page 12).

Start by couching the circle under the point where the earring finding will be sewn on. Carefully pull apart the very fine pearl purl (slightly more than you usually would) and capture one end of the wire in the centre of the circle with a couple of couching stitches. Twirl the wire around this central point and stitch three to four rows, ending by cutting the wire (with the end of the wire pointing into the fabric) and couching it down firmly.

Use another length of very fine purl (only pulled slightly apart) to outline the inner rectangular curved shape, starting at one corner. Slightly pull apart the medium width pearl purl and couch along the top outer edge and the bottom inner line of the earring template.

Thread your Jacobean thread and sew a lattice pattern in the inner enclosed curved shape, leaving diamonds measuring approximately 3 x 3 mm (⅛ x ⅛ inch). With couching thread, sew on the petite beads in the middle of each diamond.

Also sew a line of petite beads under the bottom pearl purl line (see Project 6 for sewing lines of beads). To complete the granulated effect of the beaded edging, below every three beads, sew a triangular configuration of a row of two beads and a final row of one bead.

Repeat for the other earring.

When you have finished your work, follow the instructions on page 19 for removing the work from your frame.

Cut the excess fabric, leaving about 1 cm (⅜ inch) around the outline of each earring. Trim the interfacing away from the edge of the design. Cut out two earring shapes from the piece of cardboard.

Position the goldwork design over the cardboard and flip the piece over. Carefully clip the exposed fabric so that the flaps can fold smoothly over the edge of the cardboard. Using small lengths of masking tape, catch down the flaps of the fabric over the edges of the cardboard and stick them to the back of the cardboard, folding the fabric neatly at the corners.

Once satisfied with the position of the design over the cardboard background, gently curve the cardboard so that the earrings have a bit of three-dimensional shape to them. Check your felt piece to make sure that it is slightly smaller than the cardboard shape, and using PVA or spray adhesive (sprayed onto the felt rather than the goldwork), stick the felt to the back of the cardboard. Repeat for the other earring and allow the earrings to dry (following the manufacturer's recommendations).

With tiny stitches of couching thread, attach the earring findings to the earrings. Position the stitches over the bottom of the end loops of the findings. Do not sew all round the circular loops, as this will stop the earrings swinging when they are worn. Sew a round gold bead into the centre of the loop to anchor each finding.

Store your earrings in acid-free tissue paper in a brown paper box.

PROJECT 12
Eighteenth-century French Flower Picture

Baskets of flowers were a popular decorative motif in the eighteenth and nineteenth centuries, appearing on a wide range of objects, from needlework to porcelain and furniture, including Louis XV commodes featuring deliciously asymmetrical floral marquetry designs in the best rococo taste.

YOU WILL NEED:

Standard goldwork kit (see page 20)

Special considerations for the background fabric:

Calico

Shimmering silk with a slight gradation of colour (the fabric used in the example has a lovely variegated flush of colour together with some shots of a pretty blue that I liked, as it gave an extra subtle texture to the picture)

Felt (preferably dark yellow)

Other equipment:

String about 2 mm ($\frac{1}{12}$ inch) wide dyed yellow

Couching thread:

Gold/yellow silk thread YLI #50 – 078

Goldwork metal threads:

Jap gold (#8 – medium thickness)

Pearl purl (#3 – thick)

Pearl purl (#2 – medium thickness)

Pearl purl (very fine)

Gold smooth purl (#5 – medium thickness)

Silver smooth purl (#5 – medium thickness)

Bright check (#6 – medium width)

Jacobean thread or passing thread (No 4)

Beads and other decorations:

A matt round gold glass bead approximately 6 mm ($\frac{1}{4}$ inch) diameter

A round gold pearl approximately 4 mm ($\frac{1}{6}$ inch) diameter

16 round gold beads approximately 2 mm ($\frac{1}{12}$ inch) diameter

Method

Frame up your calico and background fabric (see page 11), and trace the template (enlarge if you wish) for Project 12 onto some soft tracing paper. Once the background fabric on the frame is drum tight, transfer the design onto the fabric (see page 12).

Cut out a template from a firm piece of paper for the basket, the two flowers, the three large leaves and the bud. Attach the template onto the felt using a pin or double-sided sticky tape. Cut out a smaller round piece of felt for the centre of the large round flower. Using sharp embroidery scissors, cut out the felt around the templates.

To prepare your picture for goldwork, stab stitch (see box, page 54) the felt onto the appropriate areas of the design. For the large round flower, stab stitch the smaller round piece of felt in the centre of the first layer of felt.

Stab stitch lengths of string vertically in a ladder pattern across the surface of the padded basket, leaving 3 – 4 mm (⅛ – ⅙ inch) between them. Secure the top and bottom of each piece of string with a couple of couching stitches.

Outline your basket with the medium width pearl purl pulled slightly apart. Using a **double strand** of gold Jap, couch a row across the bottom of the basket, placing a couching stitch in between every second ladder. Make sure that each couching stitch firmly secures the double strand of gold Jap. You may wish to sew a tiny stitch into the felt near the couching stitch. Lay a second row of a double strand of gold Jap and couch this row so that the couching stitch falls in between the couching stitches of the previous row. Continue working the rows in this manner, and you will start to see that a simple but pretty basket weave will emerge. You will need to do approximately 14 rows.

Sink the ends of the Jap gold and tidy them at the back of the work. Couch a line of medium pearl purl pulled slightly apart to indicate the footing of the basket.

Next, work on the central layer of felt around the middle of the large round flower. Stitch a double loop of gold smooth purl for six petals in the middle and a triple loop of gold smooth purl for ten petals around the outside of the flower. If the entire design measures approximately 19 cm (7½ inches) x 15 cm (6 inches) the smallest petal of smooth purl measures 1.5 cm (⅝ inch), the middle length measures 2 cm (¾ inch), and the largest petal is made from 2.5 cm (1 inch) of smooth purl.

To start a loop of smooth purl, bring your threaded needle up at the point you wish the petal to start (near the middle of the flower), thread the smooth purl onto your couching thread and bring your needle down where you wish the petal to end (again near the middle of the flower).

Outline the eight-petal flower with medium pearl purl slightly pulled apart and fill each petal with silver smooth purl laid diagonally over the padding.

Outline each padded leaf with medium pearl purl slightly pulled apart. Fill the padded leaf closest to the basket with silver smooth purl, laid diagonally. Fill the largest leaf with a combination of gold smooth purl and lengths of bright check. Fill the remaining leaf with gold smooth purl.

Stitch thick pearl purl slightly pulled apart along the stems between the basket and the gold flower as well as along the main stems that flow beyond the flowers. With medium pearl purl, outline the stems and the medium-sized leaves. With fine pearl purl, outline the three smallest leaves (as well as the stem connecting the double leaves in the top right-hand corner of the design).

Fill the remaining leaves with couched lengths of Jap gold, satin stitch worked with Jacobean thread, or other varieties of stitches.

Work on the bud by outlining the shape with medium pearl purl slightly pulled apart and sewing the tip of the bud with satin stitch in Jacobean thread. For the remainder of the bud, cut small segments of bright check and sew them down randomly until they fully cover the surface of the bud.

Sew the pearl bead into the middle of the round flower and the small gold beads within the middle of each smooth purl loop. Sew the large gold bead in the middle of the silver flower.

When you have finished your work, follow the instructions on page 19 for removing the work from your frame.

Stab stitching

Stab stitching is a very simple stitch to use when securing felt pieces onto a background fabric. Thread a narrow-eyed needle with silk couching thread or a polyester thread of the same colour as the felt. Tie a knot at the end of the thread and bring the needle up through the background fabric right against one edge of the felt piece. Bring the needle down into the felt about 1 mm (1/24 inch) from the edge. The stitch should be perpendicular to the edge of the felt. Sew a stab stitch in the middle of each side of the felt and then outline the entire felt shape with small, even stab stitches 1 mm (1/24 inch) apart. A second layer of padding can be sewn down with stab stitches 2 – 3 mm (1/12 – 1/8 inch) apart.

PROJECT 13

Monsoon Wedding Paisley Motif Wedding Gift Bag

This design is taken intact from a beautiful wedding sari that had this motif machine embroidered along both edges of the generously proportioned fabric. Its delicacy and lightness appealed to me and I hope you enjoy the adaptation of the design into goldwork.

YOU WILL NEED:

Standard goldwork kit (see page 20)

Special considerations for the background fabric:

Calico

Rich white or cream silk (or a colour that matches the bride's gown)

Dark yellow felt

Other equipment:

Sewing machine to make up the rest of the bag

Couching thread:

Gold/yellow silk thread YLI #50 – 078

Goldwork metal threads:

Gold twist (3 ply – medium thickness)

Gold smooth purl (#5 – medium thickness)

Gold smooth purl (#6 – thinner wire)

Jacobean thread

Beads and other decorations:

3 pearl beads approximately 4 mm (⅙ inch) diameter

36 pearl beads approximately 2 mm (¹⁄₁₂ inch) diameter

33 ellipsoid pearls approximately 6 mm (¼ inch) long

Gold round beads approximately 2 mm (¹⁄₁₂ inch) diameter

Method

Frame up your calico and background fabric (see page 11), and trace the template for Project 13 onto some soft tracing paper. Once the background fabric on the frame is drum tight, transfer the design onto the fabric (see page 12).

Cut out a template from a firm piece of paper for the three round flowers and the four buds. Attach the template onto the felt using a pin or double-sided sticky tape. Using your sharp embroidery scissors, cut out the felt around the templates.

Stab stitch (for instructions, see page 54) the felt onto the appropriate areas of the design. Couch a **single strand** of twist along the two long stems connecting the three round flowers with the two upper buds and the two small stems flowing from either side of the bottom round flower. Couch a strand connecting the bottom central flower with the first bud.

Outline the entire outer paisley motif and the four leaf shapes at the bottom of the design with a **single stran**d of twist.

Fill in the leaf motifs with Jacobean thread worked in satin stitch. Outline each petal of each padded round flower with a 2 cm (¾ inch) loop of the medium thickness smooth purl. Outline each padded bud with three long loops (2.5 cm; 1 inch) of the same thickness smooth purl.

With a thinner smooth purl, couch five loops in a flower pattern at the end of each short stem at the bottom of the design. Using the same smooth purl thickness, make short loops (1.2 cm; ½ inch) on either side of every stem in the design, ending in an upper loop at the topmost stem. Between the border line of the paisley motif and the round flower on the right of the design, couch two buds, each made up of three loops (1.2 cm; ½ inch) of thin smooth purl. On the other side of the round flower on the left-hand side of the design, couch three small buds, using similar lengths of smooth purl.

Between the first (bottom) and second (middle) bud, couch a graduating series of lines in a 'V' formation using lengths of thin smooth purl.

Sew an ellipsoid pearl bead into each petal of the padded round flowers and the loop of the padded buds. Sew a 4 mm (⅙ inch) pearl bead in the middle of each padded flower. Sew a 2 mm (1/12 inch) pearl bead at the base of each bud, as well as in the centre of the small flowers at the end of the short stems at the bottom of the design. Also sew a 2 mm (1/12 inch) pearl bead into every loop couched along a stem.

Sew the gold beads at the top of each loop of the padded buds and into each petal of the flower at the end of the two flanking short stems at the bottom of the design. If you wish, scatter any remaining 2 mm (1/12 inch) pearl beads or gold beads in a row in any empty space.

When you have finished your work, follow the instructions on page 19 for removing the work from your frame. Use your paisley goldwork piece panel to sew a simple drawstring bag, perhaps edged with a beaded fringe, or appliqué the work onto a ready-made fabric bag.

PROJECT 14
Eclectic Goldwork Handbag

This is a fun bag to make, learning and creating goldwork spirals to decorate stripes of gorgeous fabrics. Feature spirals will be created using Jacobean thread and any other fine gold-coloured thread woven into shimmering circles of gold.

YOU WILL NEED:

Standard goldwork kit (see page 20)

Special considerations for the background fabric:

Calico

Silk, chiffon and organza fabric (eight different colours and varying textures that look attractive when arranged into a horizontally striped pattern; choose one of the fabrics to be the background for the front goldwork panel, and which will form the back of the handbag and strap connecting the front and back panels)

Satin lining (use a harmonising colour)

Thin wadding

Other equipment:

Two pieces of acid-free cardboard of medium stiffness

Masking tape

Sewing machine

Threads:

Gold/yellow silk thread YLI #50 – 078

Cotton or polyester thread that matches the base fabric

Goldwork metal threads:

Jap gold (medium thickness)

Coloured twists (to match or contrast with your chosen fabrics)

Pearl purl (#2 – medium width)

Jacobean thread or passing thread (# 4)

Thin gold braid

Beads and other decorations:

Coloured seed and other beads (to match or contrast with your chosen fabrics)

Palettes measuring from 1.8 mm (less than ⅛ inch) to 10 mm (⅜ inch)

Sequins (to match or contrast with your chosen fabrics)

Hand-dyed variegated gimp (to match or contrast with your chosen fabrics)

Method

Frame up your calico and background fabric (see page 11), and trace the template (enlarge if you wish) for Project 14 onto some soft tracing paper. On top of your background fabric, arrange your other fabrics horizontally in stripes of varying thickness, either folding the fabric strip in half or leaving a raw edge. Play with the fabric, looking for an interesting interplay between opaque and transparent fabrics. When you are pleased with the combination, stitch the fabrics in place and tighten the frame to make the fabric drum tight. Transfer the design onto the background fabric (see page 12).

Each row is designed to contain a number of spirals. You may fill each row with one of the suggested spiral patterns below or experiment with creating some spiral motifs of your own. You can incorporate your own combination of gold braid, lines of seed beads, a random scattering of larger beads or an orderly arrangement of beads sewn in between each spiral. The choice is yours.

For the sample, I sewed palettes secured by a sequin and a seed bead within the two smaller rows. For my turquoise row I couched one of my favorite pearl purl spirals — a tightly packed spiral of pearl purl that has been pulled apart slightly more than usual. Couch every second or third loop. I find this is an excellent way of using pearl purl in an item that will be used on a regular basis. Pearl purl stitched like this does not seem to catch on passing hands or fabric.

In another two rows, I stitched down an appropriate segment of colour from a strand of hand-dyed variegated gimp. I couched the gimp down with couching thread in a series of stitches that formed a wheel or pattern of spokes around the gimp. The gimp was thin enough for me to sink the central tail, and I simply cut the end of the gimp on the last spiral

and couched it down with several small stitches. With passing thread I then sewed a series of stitches forming the spokes of a wheel (effectively covering the couching thread). A gold bead in the centre completed the spiral.

For the larger circles, use a **double strand** of Jap gold and a coloured twist. Starting from the middle, couch a solid spiral until it is about 2 cm (¾ inch) wide. With Jacobean thread, sew small stitches that radiate out from the outside line of the circle. Sew seed beads sitting on a tiny palette in between the short stitches. You may then like to encircle the entire motif with a line of slightly larger palettes secured with gold or coloured seed beads.

For the main or widest fabric stripe (third stripe down in my sample), try some woven circles using Jacobean thread. To fill one of the larger stripes with a woven circle or three, sew 13 to 15 (it must be an odd number) long stitches formed as the spoke of a wheel. Work out on some tissue paper how to space them evenly around the circle and stitch them down over the tissue paper, keeping the lines fairly close into the centre, perhaps leaving clear a 4 mm (³⁄₁₆ inch) space in the centre. Bring the needle threaded with Jacobean thread up in the middle of the circle close to the end of a spoke. Weave the thread over one spoke and, working in a clockwise direction, continue weaving under and over each spoke until you have completed your circle. Outline with sequins and/or decorate with a scattering of beads. Sew a palette, sequin, large bead or a combination of these in the centre of the circle. For a finer effect you may consider weaving with DMC Fil métallisé (Art. 282 – light gold).

When you have finished your work, follow the instructions on page 19 for removing the work from your frame.

Cut the excess fabric, leaving about 1 cm (⅜ inch) around the outline of the handbag template. Cut out two handbag shapes from the cardboard and a thin layer of wadding to the handbag shape and use it to cover one of the pieces of cardboard.

Position the goldwork design over the cardboard and wadding and flip the piece over. Carefully clip the exposed fabric so that the flaps will fold smoothly over the edges of the cardboard. Using small lengths of masking tape, catch down the flaps of the fabric over the edge of the cardboard and stick them to the back of the cardboard, folding the fabric neatly at the corners.

Make a strap from your base fabric, preferably a finished width of 5–8 cm (2–3¼ inches) when finished. Adjust the strap to your desired length and form it into a continuous loop. Hand-stitch the goldwork panel onto the strap. Carefully measure and position the back panel so that it is at precisely the same position on the other edge of the strap. Your back panel may be plain or decorated with the same series of fabric strips as the front. Using the handbag template and the width of your strap as a guide, make a lining and neatly hand stitch it into the bag.

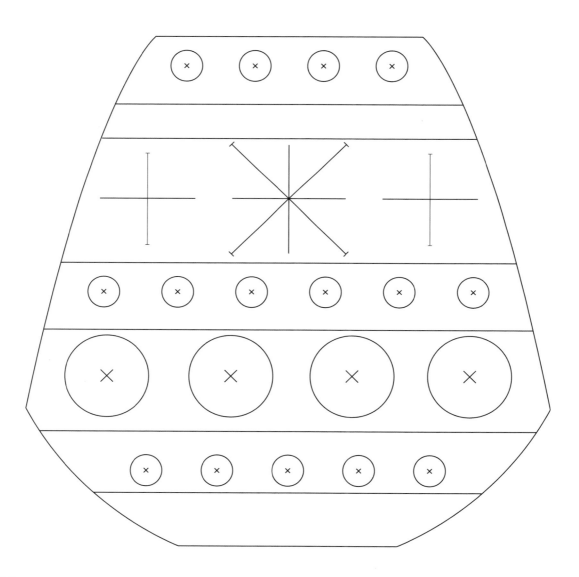

PROJECT 15
Merry Yule
Christmas Ornaments

Fun, beaded Christmas decorations can be quickly made with this simple goldwork and bead design. Enjoy finding the right combination of beads to stitch along your lines of goldwork.

YOU WILL NEED:

Standard goldwork kit (see page 20)

Special considerations for the background fabric:

Calico

A piece of lustrous silk in various shades

Felt (optional, to match the colour of your silk if you are making single-sided ornaments)

Other equipment:

Acid-free cardboard of medium stiffness

Masking tape

PVA glue or spray adhesive

Couching thread:

Gold/yellow silk thread YLI #50 – 078

Goldwork metal threads:

Jap gold (medium width)

Twist (#3 – medium width)

Beads and other decorations:

Round and faceted beads approximately 4 mm (⅙ inch) diameter; here I chose a run of five differently coloured and textured beads, each run of which contains a unifying group of beads: a round gold bead, a gold faceted and a pearl bead

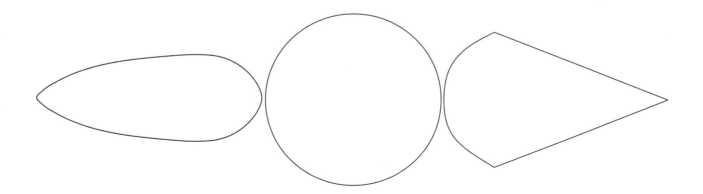

Method

Frame up your calico and background fabric (see page 11) and trace the templates (enlarge if you wish) for Project 15 from pages 61 and 62 onto some soft tracing paper. When the fabric on the frame is drum tight, transfer the design onto the fabric (see page 12). You can frame up a large piece of fabric and make more than one decoration at a time.

Start by couching a **double strand** of twist and Jap gold in a straight line along the top of your ball or cone. With the Christmas tree-shaped decoration, start with a vertical curved line and turn it so that it can start a short straight line further away from the tip of the tree template.

At the end of each line, turn the threads in a tight curve so that each line is approximately 4 mm (⅙ inch) apart to allow for the 4 mm (⅙ inch) beads. Place a couching stitch in the middle of each curve. To make a perfect turn, bring your needle up at a point 2 mm (¹⁄₁₂ inch) below the line at which you wish to make a turn. Use the needle or the couching thread to pull the goldwork threads around the corner (and to slightly ease the stiffness of the Jap gold). Bring your needle down into the fabric and secure the corner.

Choose your beads for each Christmas decoration and arrange a long row of them on either a grooved bead design board or make a long groove with a small hand towel within which the beads can rest. Pick a bright bead for the top of the Christmas tree and fill the basket at the bottom of the tree design with nine or so round gold beads.

When you have finished your work, follow the instructions on page 19 for removing the work from your frame. Finish the work by cutting the excess calico from the back of the work right to the edge of the couching. Cut the

desired Christmas shapes from the cardboard. Position the goldwork design over the cardboard and flip the piece over. Carefully clip the exposed fabric so that the flaps will fold smoothly over the edges of the cardboard. Using small lengths of masking tape, catch down the flaps of the fabric over the edge of the cardboard and stick them to the back of the cardboard, folding the fabric neatly at the corners.

The decorations can be single-sided or double-sided. If you are making a single-sided Christmas decoration, simply tape a loop of twist at the top of the ornament so that it can hang from the Christmas tree. Paste a piece of felt (cut out slightly smaller than the cardboard shape) to the back of the cardboard, using PVA or spray adhesive sprayed onto the felt rather than the goldwork. Allow the ornament to dry (following the manufacturer's instructions).

If the decoration is to be double-sided, make two identical Christmas ornaments and then place them together so that the decoration is facing out. Couch a single strand of twist along the edge between the two sides so that the two sides are sewn together, and make a loop at the top so that the decoration can be hung. Make these for your own Christmas tree or as a thoughtful Christmas present for family and friends.